the gourmet
GRILLED CHEESE
COOKBOOK
kit graham

ISBN: 978-0-9860572-0-5
thekittchen.com
Recipe Pictured on Front Cover: Artichoke, Spinach, and Red Pepper Grilled Cheese, page 11
Recipe Pictured on Back Cover: Lobster Grilled Cheese, page 51
Recipe Pictured on Title Page: Sherry, Shallot, Mushroom, and Goat Cheese Grilled Cheese, page 19
Cover Design by: Brooke Woodall (brookewoodall@gmail.com)
Email thekittchen@gmail.com for information on bulk orders.

Contents

Vegetarian 6

Meat 22

Seafood 46

Add Ins 52

Introduction

Grilled Cheese is tied to many of my memories. When I was a child, I asked my mother to make it for my lunch everyday. I loved the buttery grilled bread and gooey melted American cheese. I discovered the pairing of grilled cheese and tomato soup when I was away at summer camp. I made my husband his first ever grilled cheese on the afternoon of his 30th birthday when he asked what the melted cheese sandwiches in an advertisement were. These are just a few of the memories that inspired this book.

Grilled cheese is the ultimate comfort food. It can be simply made from bread, cheese, and butter, or it can become a gourmet meal with the addition of more sophisticated ingredients. My goal was to create recipes that transform the humble grilled cheese into a gourmet meal.

This project was funded by Kickstarter and I am endlessly grateful to those who supported the campaign that made this cookbook possible. A special thanks goes out to my friend, and favorite organic mushroom farmer, Robert Sharood of Mousam Valley Mushrooms. I would also like to thank my husband Charles for his assistance with taste testing and editing.

Before You Begin

About Grilled Cheese: Some would argue that these sandwiches are not grilled cheeses, but that they are melts. There are purists out there that believe a sandwich can only be called a grilled cheese if the only ingredients are toasted bread and melted cheese. I respectfully disagree. I also believe that melts are open-faced.

About Butter: I use grass fed butter, which is more flavorful. For perfectly crisp golden brown grilled cheese, always butter the bread, not the pan. I recommend letting the butter come to room temperature for easier spreading.

About Bread: The bread for each recipe was chosen for its texture. From lightest to most hearty the breads used in these recipes are: Challah, Italian, French, Sourdough, and Country White.

About the Recipes: The recipes are divided into four sections: Vegetarian, Meat, Seafood, and Add Ins. The Add Ins section is where you will find stand-alone recipes for items that are used in some of these grilled cheese recipes. The Add In recipes are referenced in the grilled cheese recipes, but these recipes can be enjoyed on their own and in other dishes too. The preparation time for any Add Ins is included in the total preparation time for the grilled cheese recipes that reference them.

Vegetarian

Classic Grilled Cheese with Roasted Tomato Soup 9

Artichoke, Spinach, and Red Pepper Grilled Cheese 11

K's Grilled Cheese 13

Poached Pear, Honey Roasted Walnut, and Ricotta Grilled Cheese 15

Herb Roasted Tomato and Mozzarella Grilled Cheese 17

Sherry, Shallot, Mushroom, and Goat Cheese Grilled Cheese 19

Herbed Goat Cheese and Zucchini Grilled Cheese 21

Classic Grilled Cheese with Roasted Tomato Soup

Cheddar and Monterey Jack Cheese sandwiched between toasted bread with a touch of garlic served with a creamy tomato soup.

Serves 2
Total Time: 15 minutes
Active Time: 15 minutes

For the sandwiches you will need:
4 teaspoons Butter
4 slices Country White Bread
2 slices Medium Cheddar
2 slices Monterey Jack
2 cloves Garlic

1. Spread 1 teaspoon of butter on one side of each slice of bread.

2. Assemble the sandwiches by layering 1 slice of each cheese between 2 slices of bread, buttered side facing out.

3. Place sandwiches in a large skillet over medium heat. Cover and cook for 3-4 minutes, or until golden brown. Then flip and brown the second sides of the sandwiches.

4. Gently rub the garlic over the toasted bread. The warm bread will absorb the garlic. Rub garlic on one side of the sandwiches for a subtle garlic flavor, or add garlic to both sides of the sandwiches for a more intense garlic taste.

Serves 2
Total Time: 1 hour 10 minutes
Active Time: 30 minutes

For the soup you will need:
2 tablespoons Butter
3 cups Herb Roasted Tomatoes (see page 60)
1 cup Chicken or Vegetable Broth
$1/4$ cup Heavy Cream

1. Place the roasted tomatoes in a blender and blend on the chop setting for 30 seconds. The tomatoes should be a thick and slightly chunky consistency.

2. Melt the butter in a pot over medium heat. Add the blended tomatoes.

3. Add the broth and let simmer and reduce for 20 minutes over medium-low heat.

4. Stir in the heavy cream. Serve once the soup slowly bubbles for 1 minute.

Artichoke, Spinach, and Red Pepper Grilled Cheese

Classic artichoke dip combined with provolone, spinach, and roasted red peppers.

Serves 2
Total Time: 15 minutes
Active Time: 15 minutes

You will need:
1 (14 ounce) can Artichoke Hearts
$^1/_2$ cup Mayonnaise
$^1/_2$ cup Parmesan
$^1/_4$ teaspoon Worcestershire Sauce
$^1/_4$ teaspoon Hot Sauce
4 teaspoons Butter
4 slices Italian Bread
4 slices Roasted Red Bell Pepper
(see page 65)
$^1/_3$ cup fresh Baby Spinach
2 slices Provolone

1. Chop the artichoke hearts and place in a bowl. Add the mayonnaise, Parmesan, Worcestershire Sauce, and hot sauce. Stir together.

2. In a small skillet over medium heat, bring the artichoke mixture to a slow bubble. Remove from the heat once it has bubbled for 1 minute.

3. Spread 1 teaspoon of butter on one side of each slice of bread.

4. Place 2 slices of bread on a work surface, buttered side facing down. Spread $^1/_2$ cup of the artichoke mixture on top each of the 2 slices of bread. Add a layer of roasted red bell pepper and a handful of spinach on top of the artichoke mixture.

5. Place a slice of provolone over the spinach. Finish assembling the sandwiches by adding the second slices of bread on top of the provolone, buttered side facing out.

6. Place sandwiches in a large skillet over medium heat. Cover and cook for 3-4 minutes, or until golden brown. Then flip and brown the second sides of the sandwiches.

K's Grilled Cheese
Sautéed mushrooms and roasted garlic with mellow munster cheese.

Serves 2
Total Time: 1 hour
Active Time: 15 minutes

You will need:
1 teaspoon Olive Oil
6 teaspoons Butter
8 ounces sliced Cremini Mushrooms
$1/4$ teaspoon Salt
$1/8$ teaspoon Pepper
4 slices Country White Bread
4-6 cloves of Roasted Garlic (see page 64)
4 slices Munster

1. Heat the olive oil and 2 teaspoons of butter in a skillet over medium heat. Once the butter has melted, add the mushrooms, salt, and pepper. Stir together until the mushrooms are evenly coated in the butter and olive oil. Sauté for 6 minutes, or until the mushrooms have browned.

2. Spread 1 teaspoon of butter on one side of each slice of bread.

3. Place 2 slices of bread on a work surface, buttered side facing down. Spread 2-3 cloves of roasted garlic on each slice of bread. Layer a slice of munster, the mushrooms, and another slice of munster on top. Place second slices of bread over the munster, buttered sided facing out.

4. Place sandwiches in a large clean skillet over medium heat. Cover and cook for 3-4 minutes, or until golden brown. Then flip and brown the second sides of the sandwiches.

Poached Pear, Honey Roasted Walnut, and Homemade Ricotta Grilled Cheese

A slightly sweet sandwich with creamy fresh ricotta cheese.

Serves 2
Total Time: 45 minutes
Active Time: 45 minutes

You will need:
4 teaspoons Butter
4 slices Sourdough Bread
$1/_2$ cup Homemade Ricotta (see page 61)
$1/_2$ cup Marsala Poached Pears (see page 63)
4 tablespoons Honey Roasted Walnuts (see page 62)

1. Spread 1 teaspoon of butter on one side of each slice of bread.

2. Place the slices of bread on a work surface, buttered side facing down. Spread ricotta on each slice of bread.

3. Spread the pears and then the walnuts on 2 of the slices of bread, on top of the ricotta. Finish assembling the sandwiches by adding the second slice of bread to each sandwich, ricotta side facing down.

4. Place sandwiches in a large skillet over medium heat. Cover and cook for 3-4 minutes, or until golden brown. Then flip and brown the second sides of the sandwiches.

Herb Roasted Tomato and Mozzarella Grilled Cheese

Tomatoes roasted with oregano and basil paired with fresh mozzarella and spinach.

Serves 2
Total Time: 1 hour
Active Time: 15 minutes

You will need:
4 teaspoons Butter
4 slices Italian Bread
$1/2$ cup Herb Roasted Tomatoes (see page 60)
1 medium ball of fresh Mozzarella, sliced
$1/2$ cup Spinach

1. Spread 1 teaspoon of butter on one side of each slice of bread.

2. Place 2 slices of bread on a work surface, buttered side facing down. Layer the roasted tomatoes, the mozzarella slices, and the spinach on top of each slice of bread. Then top with the second slices of bread, buttered side facing out.

3. Place sandwiches in a large skillet over medium heat. Cover and cook for 3-4 minutes, or until golden brown. Then flip and brown the second sides of the sandwiches.

Sherry, Shallot, Mushroom, and Goat Cheese Grilled Cheese

Mushrooms and shallots sautéed in Sherry with melted goat cheese and a Parmesan crust.

Serves 2
Total Time: 20 minutes
Active Time: 20 minutes

You will need:
4 teaspoons, plus 1 tablespoon Butter
4 teaspoons shredded Parmesan
1 small Shallot, sliced
$1/2$ cup sliced Cremini Mushrooms
$1/2$ cup sliced Oyster Mushrooms
$1/2$ cup sliced Shiitake Mushrooms
$1/4$ teaspoon Salt
$1/8$ teaspoon Pepper
$1/3$ cup Sherry
8 tablespoons Goat Cheese, at room temperature
$1/3$ cup Spinach
4 slices Italian Bread

1. Spread 1 teaspoon of butter one side of each slice of bread. Spread 1 teaspoon of Parmesan over the butter and lightly press it into the bread.

2. Melt 1 tablespoon of butter in a skillet over medium heat. Add the shallot, mushrooms, salt, and pepper. Toss together until the mushrooms and shallots are evenly coated in the butter. Cook for 2 minutes. Then add the sherry. Sauté for 6 minutes, or until the mushrooms have browned.

3. Place the slices of bread on a work surface, Parmesan side facing down. Spread 2 tablespoons of goat cheese on top of each slice of bread.

4. Add the sautéed mushrooms and shallots on top of 2 of the slices of bread. Add the spinach on top. Place the second slices of bread on top of the spinach, Parmesan side facing out.

5. Heat a clean skillet over medium-high heat. Place the sandwiches in the ungreased skillet and toast for about 3 minutes a side, until the bread and Parmesan cheese is golden brown. Flip and brown the second sides of the sandwiches.

Herbed Goat Cheese and Zucchini Grilled Cheese

Goat cheese seasoned with roasted red pepper, basil, and oregano paired with sautéed zucchini slices.

Serves 2
Total Time: 20 minutes
Active Time: 20 minutes

You will need:
8 tablespoons Goat Cheese, at room temperature
1 tablespoon chopped Basil
1 tablespoon chopped Oregano
3 tablespoons diced Roasted Red Bell Pepper (see page 65)
2 Zucchinis, sliced lengthwise
2 teaspoons Olive Oil
$1/4$ teaspoon Salt
$1/8$ teaspoon Pepper
4 teaspoons Butter
4 slices Country White Bread

1. Stir the goat cheese, basil, oregano, and roasted red bell pepper together. Set aside.

2. In a large bowl, toss the zucchini in the olive oil, salt, and pepper. Heat a skillet or grill pan over high heat and add the seasoned zucchini. Cook the zucchini for about 4 minutes per side, or until browned.

3. Spread 1 teaspoon of butter on one side of each slice of bread.

4. Place the slices of bread on a work surface, buttered side facing down. Spread 2 tablespoons of the herbed goat cheese on the top of each slice of bread.

5. Layer zucchini slices on top of 2 of the slices of bread. Then add the second slices of bread on top of the zucchini, goat cheese side facing down.

6. Place sandwiches in a large skillet over medium heat. Cover and cook for 3-4 minutes, or until golden brown. Then flip and brown the second sides of the sandwiches.

Meat

Chicken Parmesan Grilled Cheese 25

Buffalo Chicken and Blue Cheese Grilled Cheese 27

Bacon Guacamole Grilled Cheese 29

Spicy Italian Sausage Grilled Cheese 31

Creamy Spinach, Bacon, and Mushroom Grilled Cheese...............33

The Hanna 35

Turkey, Pesto, and Provolone Grilled Cheese with Sundried Tomatoes 37

Melanie's Joy Grilled Cheese 39

Jalapeño Popper Grilled Cheese 41

Roast Beef, Mushroom, Brie, and Caramelized Onion Grilled Cheese...... 43

Loaded Baked Potato Grilled Cheese..45

Chicken Parmesan Grilled Cheese

Crunchy panko coated chicken topped with fresh mozzarella and roasted tomatoes.

Serves 2
Total Time: 1 hour
Active Time: 30 minutes

You will need:
4 teaspoons Butter
4 slices Italian Bread
4 tablespoons Homemade Ricotta (see page 61)
2 pieces of Chicken Parmesan (see page 55)
4 fresh Basil Leaves

1. Spread 1 teaspoon of butter on one side of each slice of bread.

2. Place 2 slices of bread on a work surface, buttered side facing down. Spread 2 tablespoons of ricotta on top of the slices of bread.

3. Layer a warm piece of Chicken Parmesan (topped with the herb roasted tomatoes and slice of mozzarella according to the recipe), and 2 basil leaves on top of the ricotta. Then add the second slices of bread to the sandwiches, buttered side facing out.

4. Place sandwiches in a large skillet over medium heat. Cover and cook for 3-4 minutes, or until golden brown. Then flip and brown the second sides of the sandwiches.

Buffalo Chicken and Blue Cheese Grilled Cheese

The spiciness of slow cooked buffalo chicken is balanced by cream cheese and blue cheese.

Serves 2
Total Time: 6 hours, 30 minutes
Active Time: 30 minutes

You will need:
1 (23 ounce) bottle of Hot Sauce (such as Frank's Red Hot)
1 packet dry Ranch dressing
1 $^1/_2$ pounds Chicken Thighs
4 slices Country White Bread
4 teaspoons Butter
4 tablespoons Cream Cheese, at room temperature
4 tablespoons Blue Cheese

30 minute Shortcut:
Start with a cooked rotisserie chicken, shred the meat, and stir in $^1/_2$ cup of hot sauce. Skip to step 3.

1. In a slow cooker whisk together the hot sauce and ranch dressing. Add the chicken thighs and set the slow cooker on to low. Cook for 6 hours. For best results, make sure that the hot sauce completely covers the chicken thighs.

2. Remove the chicken from the slow cooker and place in a bowl. Use a fork to shred. The chicken will have absorbed some of the hot sauce and will be mildly spicy. For spicier chicken, add some of the remaining hot sauce from the slow cooker to the chicken.

3. Spread 1 teaspoon of butter on one side of each slice of bread. Place the slices of bread on a work surface, buttered side facing down.

4. Spread 1 tablespoon of cream cheese on the other side of each slice of bread. Layer $^1/_4$ cup of the shredded chicken and two tablespoons blue cheese on 2 of the slices of bread and top with the second slices of bread, buttered side facing out.

5. Place sandwiches in a large skillet over medium heat. Cover and cook for 3-4 minutes, or until golden brown. Then flip and brown the second sides of the sandwiches.

Bacon Guacamole Grilled Cheese

Poblano peppers add a smoky hint of spice to the guacamole in this grilled cheese.

Serves 2
Total Time: 30 minutes
Active Time: 10 minutes

You will need:
4 teaspoons Butter
4 slices Sourdough Bread
$1/2$ cup Guacamole, (see page 59)
4 slices of Bacon, cut in half and cooked (see page 66)
4 slices Medium Cheddar

1. Spread 1 teaspoon of butter on one side of each slice of bread.

2. Spread $1/4$ cup guacamole on the other side of 2 the slices of bread.

3. Place 4 half-slices of bacon and 2 slices of cheese on top of the guacamole. Then top with the second slices of bread, buttered side facing out.

4. Place sandwiches in a large skillet over medium heat. Cover and cook for 3-4 minutes, or until golden brown. Then flip and brown the second sides of the sandwiches.

Spicy Italian Sausage Grilled Cheese
A hearty sandwich with provolone, roasted red bell peppers, and spinach.

Serves 2
Total Time: 30 minutes
Active Time: 30 minutes

You will need:
2 Spicy Italian Sausages
4 slices Italian Bread
4 teaspoons Butter
4 slices Provolone
1/2 cup Baby Spinach
4 slices Roasted Red Bell Pepper (see page 65)

1. Slice the sausage in half lengthwise. Heat a skillet or grill pan over medium heat. Add the 4 slices of sausage. Cover and cook first side for 6 minutes. Flip and cook second side for 6 minutes. The sausage is fully cooked when it is no longer red in the center and has reached 145 degrees.

2. Spread 1 teaspoon of butter on one side of each slice of bread.

3. Place 2 of the slices of bread on a work surface, buttered side facing down. Assemble the sandwiches by layering 1 sausage, 2 slices of provolone, 1/4 cup spinach and 2 slices of roasted pepper on top of the slices of bread. Then add the second slices of bread to the sandwiches, buttered side facing out.

4. Place sandwiches in a large clean skillet over medium heat. Cover and cook for 3-4 minutes, or until golden brown. Then flip and brown the second sides of the sandwiches.

Creamy Spinach, Bacon, and Mushroom Grilled Cheese

Creamy cheesy spinach, sautéed portabella mushroom slices, bacon, and provolone.

Serves 2
Total Time: 30 minutes
Active Time: 20 minutes

You will need:
1 tablespoon plus 4 teaspoons Butter
2 Portabella Mushrooms, sliced
1/4 teaspoon Salt
1/8 teaspoon Pepper
1/4 cup White Wine
1 tablespoon Olive Oil
1 pound fresh Baby Spinach
1/4 cup Parmesan
1/4 cup Goat Cheese
4 slices Italian Bread
2 slices Provolone
4 slices Bacon, cut in half and cooked (see page 66)

1. Melt 1 tablespoon of butter in a skillet over medium heat. Add the mushrooms, salt, and pepper. Stir until the mushrooms are evenly coated in butter. Add the white wine. Sauté the mushrooms for 6 minutes, or until browned. Set aside.

2. Heat the olive oil in a skillet over medium-low heat. Add the spinach, Parmesan, and goat cheese. Cover with a lid. Cook until the cheese has melted and the spinach has wilted, about 3 minutes. Stir thoroughly.

3. Spread 1 teaspoon of butter on one side of each slice of bread.

4. Place 2 slices of bread on a work surface, buttered side facing down. Layer a slice of provolone, half the spinach, half the mushrooms, 4 half-slices of bacon, and another slice of provolone on each slice of bread. Add the second slices of bread on top of the provolone, buttered side facing out.

5. Place sandwiches in a large skillet over medium heat. Cover and cook for 3-4 minutes, or until golden brown. Then flip and brown the second sides of the sandwiches.

The Hanna

A sweet and savory grilled cheese with prosciutto, Gorgonzola, mozzarella, and honey roasted walnuts.

Serves 2
Total Time: 20 minutes
Active Time: 15 minutes

You will need:
4 slices of Country White Bread
1 medium ball fresh Mozzarella, sliced
8 slices of Prosciutto
4 tablespoons Honey Roasted Walnuts (see page 62)
4 tablespoons crumbled Gorgonzola
1 teaspoon Truffle Oil
1 tablespoon Olive Oil

1. Place 2 slices of bread on a work surface. Layer the half of the mozzarella, 4 slices of prosciutto, 2 tablespoons walnuts, and 2 tablespoons Gorgonzola on each slice of bread. Top with the second slices of bread.

2. Mix the truffle oil and olive oil together in a small bowl.

3. Heat half of the oil in a skillet over medium heat. Add the sandwiches, and cover the skillet. Cook the first side of the sandwiches for 3-4 minutes, or until golden brown. Then remove the sandwiches from the skillet. Heat the remaining oil in the skillet and brown the second sides of the sandwiches.

Turkey, Pesto, and Provolone Grilled Cheese with Sundried Tomatoes

An Italian inspired grilled cheese with bold flavors.

Serves 2
Total Time: 10 minutes
Active Time: 10 minutes

You will need:
4 slices Italian Bread
4 teaspoons Butter
4 tablespoons Pesto
4 slices Provolone
6 slices Roast Turkey
8-10 slices Sundried Tomatoes

1. Spread 1 teaspoon of butter on one side of each slice of bread.

2. Place the slices of bread on a work surface, buttered side facing down. Spread 1 tablespoon of pesto on each slice of bread.

3. Layer a slice of provolone, 3 slices of turkey, the sundried tomatoes, another slice of provolone on 2 of the slices of bread. Finish assembling the sandwiches by adding the second slices of bread on top of the provolone, buttered side facing out.

4. Place sandwiches in a large skillet over medium heat. Cover and cook for 3-4 minutes, or until golden brown. Then flip and brown the second sides of the sandwiches.

Melanie's Joy Grilled Cheese

A sandwich made with fried Brie, cranberry chutney, roasted almonds, and turkey.

Serves 2
Total Time: 25 minutes
Active Time: 25 minutes

You will need:
$1/4$ cup Sliced Almonds
4 slices Country White Bread
4 teaspoons Butter
8 slices Roast Turkey
4 tablespoons Cranberry Chutney (see page 56)
1 wedge Fried Brie (see page 58)

1. Pour the sliced almonds on a baking sheet and bake at 350 degrees for 2-3 minutes, until just brown. Set aside.

2. Spread 1 teaspoon of butter on one side of each slice of bread.

3. Toast the buttered side of bread in a grill pan or skillet and set aside.

4. Place 2 slices of bread on a work surface, toasted side facing down. Layer 2 tablespoons of the cranberry chutney, half of the roasted almonds, and 4 slices of turkey on top.

5. Fry the Brie according to the directions on page 58. Once fried, let cool for 3 minutes, and then slice. Place half of the Brie on each sandwich. Top with the second slice of bread, grilled side facing out, and serve.

Jalapeño Popper Grilled Cheese

Spicy roasted jalapeños with blend of Mexican cheese, cream cheese, and bacon.

Serves 2
Total Time: 35 minutes
Active Time: 15 minutes

You will need:
6 Jalapeño Peppers
4 slices Country White Bread
4 teaspoons Butter
4 tablespoons Cream Cheese
4 slices Bacon, cut in half and cooked (see page 66)
$1/4$ cup Shredded Mexican Cheese

1. Cut the stems off the jalapeños and slice the peppers in half lengthwise. Bake for 15 minutes at 400 degrees.

2. Once the peppers have cooled, use a knife to scrape out the seeds and membranes. Loosely chop.

3. Spread 1 teaspoon of butter on one side of each slice of bread.

4. Place the slices of bread on a work surface, buttered side facing down. Spread 1 tablespoon of cream cheese on each slice of bread.

5. Layer the chopped jalapeños, 4 half-slices of bacon, and shredded cheese on 2 of the slices of bread. Top with the second slices of bread, buttered side facing out.

6. Place sandwiches in a large skillet over medium heat. Cover and cook for 3-4 minutes, or until golden brown. Then flip and brown the second sides of the sandwiches.

Roast Beef, Mushroom, Brie, and Caramelized Onion Grilled Cheese

A grilled cheese with rich and robust flavors.

Serves 2
Total Time: 40 minutes
Active Time: 40 minutes

You will need:
2 tablespoons Olive Oil
1 large Yellow Onion, sliced
2 Portabella Mushrooms, sliced
6 teaspoons Butter
4 slices French Bread
6 slices Roast Beef
4 slices cut from a wedge of Brie
$1/4$ cup Spinach

1. Heat the olive oil in a saucepan over low heat. Add the onion, and sauté for 30 minutes, or until the onions are golden brown. Stir frequently.

2. Meanwhile, melt 2 teaspoons of butter in a skillet over medium heat. Stir in the mushrooms and sauté for 6 minutes, or until golden brown.

3. Spread 1 teaspoon of butter on one side of each slice of bread.

4. Place 2 slices of bread on a work surface, buttered side facing down. Layer the roast beef, Brie, spinach, mushrooms, and caramelized onions on the slices of bread. Then add the second slices of bread on top, buttered side facing out.

5. Place sandwiches in a large clean skillet over medium heat. Cover and cook for 3-4 minutes, or until golden brown. Then flip and brown the second sides of the sandwiches.

Loaded Baked Potato Grilled Cheese

Crisp roasted potatoes topped with cheese, bacon, chive sour cream, and tomato.

Serves 2
Total Time: 50 minutes
Active Time: 50 minutes

You will need:
4 tablespoons Sour Cream
$1/2$ teaspoon chopped Chives
4 slices Country White Bread
4 teaspoons Butter
6 slices Crispy Potatoes (see page 57)
4 slices Bacon, cut in half and cooked (see page 66)
1 Tomato, sliced
4 slices Medium Cheddar

1. Stir the sour cream and chives together.

2. Spread 1 teaspoon of butter on one side of each slice of bread.

3. Place 2 slices of bread on a work surface, buttered side facing down. Spread the chive sour cream on the slices of bread. Then layer 3 slices of crispy potatoes, 4 half-slices of bacon, 2 slices of tomato, and 2 slices of cheddar on top of the sour cream. Then add the second slices of bread to the sandwiches, buttered side facing out.

4. Place sandwiches in a large skillet over medium heat. Cover and cook for 3-4 minutes, or until golden brown. Then flip and brown the second sides of the sandwiches.

Seafood

Calvin's Crab Rangoon Grilled Cheese 49

Lobster Grilled Cheese 51

Calvin's Crab Rangoon Grilled Cheese
The crabmeat and cream cheese appetizer transformed into a sandwich.

Serves 2
Total Time: 20 minutes
Active Time: 20 minutes

You will need:
4 tablespoons Cream Cheese
2 tablespoons Sour Cream
$1/4$ teaspoon Soy Sauce
2 teaspoons chopped Chives
$1/4$ teaspoon Sugar
1 clove Garlic, crushed
$1/2$ cup Crabmeat
4 teaspoons Butter
4 slices Country White Bread

1. Stir the cream cheese, sour cream, and soy sauce together.

2. Add the chives, sugar, garlic, and crabmeat. Stir.

3. Heat in a skillet over medium-low heat until warm.

4. Spread 1 teaspoon of butter on one side of each slice of bread.

5. Spread the warm crab mixture on the opposite side of 2 slices of bread, and then top with the second slices of bread, buttered side facing out.

6. Place sandwiches in a large skillet over medium heat. Cover and cook for 3-4 minutes, or until golden brown. Then flip and brown the second sides of the sandwiches.

Lobster Grilled Cheese
A decadent poached lobster sandwich with a creamy cheese sauce.

Serves 2
Total Time: 20 minutes
Active Time: 20 minutes

You will need:
1/3 cup Whole Milk
1 teaspoon Flour
5 tablespoons shredded Cheddar
5 tablespoons shredded Gruyere
1 teaspoon chopped fresh Parsley
2 tablespoons, plus 4 teaspoons Butter
1/4 cup White Wine
1 small Shallot, sliced
2 Lobster Tails (fresh or thawed)
4 slices Challah Bread
1 slice Lemon

1. Whisk the milk and flour together in a small saucepan over medium heat. Stir constantly and bring to a slow boil for 1 minute to thicken. Then add 4 tablespoons of each cheese and stir until melted. Stir in the parsley. Keep warm.

2. Cut a slit through the top of the shell to the base of the lobster tails.

3. Heat 2 tablespoons of butter and the white wine in a small skillet over medium heat. Add the shallot. Once fragrant, add the lobster tails. Cook each side for 2 minutes while spooning the butter sauce over the lobster tails.

4. Remove lobster meat from the shell. Remove the black vein (the intestine) that runs down the tail. The meat should be almost fully cooked. Loosely dice the meat. Add the meat to the warm cheese sauce; cook for 1 minute or until lobster meat is no longer translucent.

5. Spread 1 teaspoon of butter on one side of the slices of bread. Spread 1 tablespoon of cheddar on the other side of 2 slices of bread. Place the lobster on top and spoon cheese sauce over. Squeeze the lemon over. Sprinkle 1 tablespoon of Gruyere over the lobster and then top with second slices of bread, buttered side facing out.

6. Place sandwiches in a large skillet over medium heat. Cover and cook for 3-4 minutes, or until golden brown. Then flip and brown the second sides of the sandwiches.

Add Ins

Artichoke Dip 54

Chicken Parmesan 55

Cranberry Chutney 56

Crispy Roasted Potatoes...57

Fried Brie 58

Guacamole 59

Herb Roasted Tomatoes... 60

Homemade Ricotta 61

Honey Roasted Walnuts... 62

Marsala Poached Pears 63

Roasted Garlic 64

Roasted Peppers 65

Perfectly Cooked Bacon... 66

Artichoke Dip

This creamy cheesy dip with chunks of artichoke can be added to grilled cheese or enjoyed as an appetizer.

You will need:
2 cans Artichoke Hearts
1 cup Mayonnaise
1 cup Parmesan
$^1/_4$ teaspoon Worcestershire sauce
$^1/_4$ teaspoon Hot Sauce

1. Chop the artichoke hearts and place in a bowl. Add all the other ingredients and stir together.

2. Bake at 350 degrees for 40 minutes. Serve with crackers or chips.

Serves 6
Total Time: 45 minutes
Active Time: 5 minutes

Chicken Parmesan

An easy to prepare version of the Italian classic served with roasted tomatoes.

Serves 4
Total Time: 50 minutes
Active Time: 30 minutes

You will need:
1 $1/2$ cups Italian Seasoned Panko
$1/2$ cup shredded Parmesan
3 Eggs
1 pound thinly cut Chicken Breasts
2 tablespoons Olive Oil
1 slice fresh Mozzarella per slice of Chicken Breast
1 cup Herb Roasted Tomatoes (see page 60)

1. Combine the panko and Parmesan in a bowl. Beat the eggs in another bowl.

2. Dredge the chicken in the panko mixture, then in the egg, and then in the panko again.

3. Heat 1 tablespoon of olive oil in a skillet. Brown the first side chicken, cooking for 4 minutes, or until browned. Then flip and add the rest of the olive oil to the pan. Cook second side of the chicken until browned.

4. Place the chicken on a baking sheet and bake at 350 degrees for 15 minutes, or until the center of the chicken is no longer pink.

5. Top the chicken with fresh mozzarella and warm roasted tomatoes.

Cranberry Chutney

A bold combination of sweet and bitter that pairs perfectly with Fried Brie.

You will need:
1 tablespoon Olive Oil
2 Shallots, sliced
$1/2$ cup Frozen Cranberries
2 tablespoons Cider Vinegar
$1/8$ teaspoon Salt
$1/8$ teaspoon Pepper
3 tablespoons Sugar

1. Heat the olive oil in a small saucepan over medium heat. Add shallots cook for 3 minutes.

2. Add all the other ingredients. Stir together. Bring to a simmer. Let simmer and reduce on low heat for 10 minutes stirring frequently. The chutney will be thick and syrupy when done.

Serves 4
Total Time: 15 minutes
Active Time: 15 minutes

Crispy Roasted Potatoes
Thin crispy slices of herb-seasoned potato are a quick and easy side dish.

Serves 2
Total Time: 50 minutes
Active Time: 10 minutes

You will need:
1 large Yukon Gold Potato
1 tablespoon Olive Oil
1 tablespoon Butter, melted
1 teaspoon chopped Oregano
1 teaspoon chopped Basil
1 clove Garlic, minced
$1/4$ teaspoon Salt
$1/8$ teaspoon Pepper

1. Heat oven to 400 degrees. Cut the potatoes lengthwise into slices $1/8$ inch thick.

2. Toss all of the ingredients together in a large bowl, until the potatoes are evenly coated with the herbs, butter, and olive oil.

3. Spread the potatoes out in a single layer on a baking sheet. Bake for 15-20 minutes, or until the bottom sides of the potato slices have browned.

4. Flip the potatoes, and cook for another 10 minutes, or until the second sides brown.

Fried Brie

Creamy Brie fried with a crispy panko crust that can be paired with cranberry chutney and served as an appetizer.

You will need:
1 Egg
$^1/_2$ cup Panko
1 wedge of Brie, chilled
2 tablespoons Olive Oil

1. Beat the egg in a shallow bowl. Pour the panko into a shallow bowl.

2. Dredge the Brie in the egg, and then in the panko. Repeat, dredging the Brie in the egg and panko again. Press the panko into the Brie, forming a thick layer around the cheese.

3. Heat the olive oil in a skillet over medium-high heat. Add the panko coated Brie. Toast each side for 1-2 minutes, or until golden brown.

Serves 6
Total Time: 10 minutes
Active Time: 10 minutes

Guacamole
A spicy guacamole with roasted poblano peppers and a touch of citrus.

Serves 4
Total Time: 30 minutes
Active Time: 30 minutes

You will need:
1 slice of a quartered Lemon
1 slice of a quartered Lime
1 Avocado, pitted and diced
$1/8$ teaspoon Salt
1 tablespoon finely chopped Red Onion
3 tablespoons diced Roasted Poblano Pepper
(see page 65)
$1/4$ cup chopped Tomato, any variety

1. Squeeze the juice from the lemon and lime wedges into a small bowl. Use a fork to remove any seeds.

2. Add the avocado and salt to the bowl of lemon and lime juice. Mash ingredients together with a fork or potato masher. Mash until the avocado reaches the consistently you desire.

3. Stir in the red onion, poblano pepper, and tomato.

4. Serve with tortilla chips, add to sandwiches, or use as a taco topping.

Herb Roasted Tomatoes

Tomatoes seasoned with basil, oregano, garlic, and olive oil can be used to make soup, added to sandwiches, or served over pasta.

You will need:
3 cups diced Tomatoes, any variety
2 tablespoons Olive Oil
2 cloves Garlic, minced
1 tablespoon Oregano, finely chopped
1 tablespoon Basil, finely chopped
$1/4$ teaspoon Salt
$1/8$ teaspoon Pepper

1. Heat oven to 350 degrees. Place the tomatoes in a large baking dish.

2. Add the olive oil, garlic, oregano, basil, salt, and pepper to the baking dish. Stir until the herbs are evenly distributed.

3. Bake for 30 -40 minutes. The tomatoes should be soft and most of the liquid from the tomatoes should have evaporated.

Serves 4-6
Total Time: 50 minutes
Active Time: 10 minutes

Homemade Ricotta

Freshly made ricotta is thick, creamy, and surprisingly easy to prepare.

Serves 6
Total Time: 25 minutes
Active Time: 10 minutes

You will need:
2 cups Whole Milk
1 cup Heavy Cream
$1/2$ teaspoon Salt
1 $1/2$ tablespoons White Wine Vinegar
Cheesecloth

1. Stir the milk, cream, and salt together in a saucepan, and bring to a full boil over medium heat.

2. Once the mixture reaches a boil, turn off the heat. Add the vinegar and let the cheese curdle for 1 minute.

3. Line a colander with 2 layers of cheesecloth.

4. Pour the ricotta through the cheesecloth-lined colander. Let sit and drain for at least 30 minutes. The longer the ricotta drains, the thicker it will be. Refrigerate in an airtight container. The ricotta will keep for 2 days.

Honey Roasted Walnuts

Sweet honey roasted walnuts with just a hint of cayenne pepper can also be added to a cheese plate or served as a snack.

You will need:
$1/4$ cup Honey
$1 1/2$ tablespoons Sugar
$1/8$ teaspoon Cayenne Pepper
1 cup Walnut Pieces

1. Melt the honey, sugar, and cayenne pepper together over medium heat in a small saucepan.

2. Remove from heat, and stir in the walnuts.

3. Strain excess honey off the walnuts.

4. Spread the walnuts out in a single layer on a baking sheet. Bake at 350 degrees for 7 minutes.

Serves 6
Total Time: 15 minutes
Active Time: 5 minutes

Marsala Poached Pears

Pears poached in rich Marsala wine and butter are a great addition to a salad or sandwich.

You will need:
1 tablespoon Butter
1 Bartlett Pear, sliced
$1/2$ cup Dry Marsala Wine

1. Melt the butter in a skillet over medium-low heat; add the pears. Stir and cook for 2 minutes. Then add the wine. Bring to a low simmer.

2. Cook for about 15 minutes, or until the liquid is absorbed and the pears are translucent.

Serves 2
Total Time: 20 minutes
Active Time: 20 minutes

Roasted Garlic

Oven roasted garlic is easy to spread and can be added to pasta, sandwiches, or mashed potatoes.

You will need:
1 head of Garlic
2 teaspoons Olive Oil

1. Slice the top off the head of garlic and place it head down in a muffin pan. Pour 2 teaspoons olive oil over the garlic. Place aluminum foil over the garlic. Bake at 400 degrees for 30 minutes.

2. Remove the garlic from the oven. Let cool, and then use a fork to remove the roasted garlic cloves from the head of garlic.

Serves 6
Total Time: 35 minutes
Active Time: 5 minutes

Roasted Peppers

Simple steps to prepare roasted peppers either using a stovetop flame or an oven.

Serves 2
Total Time: 25 minutes
Active Time: 15 minutes

You will need:
1 Pepper, any variety

1. Gas stove method: Turn on a burner. Use tongs to place the pepper directly over the flame. Rotate every couple of minutes until the skin of the pepper is charred.

Oven method: Slice the pepper into 4 or 5 large pieces. Spread the peppers out on a baking sheet, skin facing up. Roast for 15 minutes at 500 degrees until the skin of the peppers is charred.

2. Immediately place the peppers in a bowl and cover the bowl with plastic wrap. The steam that forms helps to separate the skin from the pepper.

3. Let the peppers come down to room temperature. Cut the pepper into 4-5 pieces if you used the gas stove method. Then peel the skin off the peppers under running water.

Perfectly Cooked Bacon
The easiest way to prepare evenly crisped bacon is to bake it in the oven.

You will need:
Bacon

1. Heat oven to 400 degrees.

2. Slice the bacon in half widthwise, so that it will easily fit into a sandwich.

3. Line a baking sheet with aluminum foil. It is important to use a baking sheet that has edges. Spread the bacon out in a single layer on the aluminum foil.

4. Bake for 15-20 minutes, until the bacon has reached the desired amount of crispness.

5. Remove bacon from the oven, and place on a plate or cooking rack. Use a paper towel to blot extra grease.

Serving size: 2 slices per sandwich
Total Time: 20 minutes
Active Time: 5 minutes

About the Author

Kit Graham writes thekittchen.com, a food site focused on original and practical recipes. The Kittchen has been featured on Refinery 29, Eater, The Frisky, and The Urbaness. Kit grew up in Kennebunk, Maine and currently resides in Chicago with her husband.

CPSIA information can be obtained at www.ICGtesting.com
Printed in the USA
BVIW12n1719040615
403008BV00004B/10